RESTORED

Connecting with God
After Divorce

SHAUNTAE SPAULDING

SPIRITUAL GROWTH MINISTRIES

RESTORED

I want to thank God for restoring my life when I thought it was over and to my wonderful son, who has continued to support and encourage me every day of my life.

DEVOTIONAL TITLES

Plan B

Don't Run Away

Let It Flow

He Lights the Way

Stop Worrying

Not My Enemy

He Does Care

Falling Everyday

Run, Jump, Hide

Bought at a Price

What You Wearin'?

Not Here to Please

Keeping His Commands

Keep Doing Good

Spending Time Wisely

Bring it On

Guard Your Heart

Stop the Hate

Jealous of Who?

Unload Forgiveness

Strength and Honor

His Masterpiece

His Healing Power

Enough Crying

Stay Productive

Living for Him

Know Him Better

Stay Prayerful

Hold on Tight

Reflection of Him

ACKNOWLEDGEMENT

I want to thank you for your support in purchasing my book. I pray this book will help you as you begin to start your life over. My hope to you is that you will use this book as a guide in restoring your Faith and building a stronger relationship with Jesus. Life can be difficult and going through a divorce can be challenging, confusing and for some, exciting. Whatever your divorce represents, it is not the end. God has more in store for you! A relationship that you may have spent years or even months, has now come to an end and you may be wondering where to start. Start with Jesus. Let him put you back together again. This book will help you realize that you are more than a divorcee, you are a Child of God. You matter to God more than you know. The pain and tears you have shed may not go away quickly, but by reading the Scriptures I have selected in this book, you will grow to accept what has been done and move on and connect with God. God has not forgotten you or forsaken you! As you connect with God during this time it will be an emotional and joyous journey of finding yourself again and walking with the One who knows you best!

I would love to hear about your journey and how this book has helped you. Please feel free to connect with me on my website: www.spiritualgrowthministries.com follow me on Instagram @spiritual_growth_min or email me at: spiritualgrowthmin@gmail.com

INTRODUCTION

I still remember the day I decided to divorce my husband. It was a warm, sunny Saturday afternoon and we were planning on going to the mall with our son. Right before we were supposed to leave, we got into an argument. His curse words pierced my heart too many times and the last blow was seeing my two year old son listening to it all. I was DONE! I ran into the bedroom and cried for hours. I was tired of feeling like a doormat and I didn't want my son to think the same. Divorce seemed like the only option.

After the divorce, I held on to baggage that was destroying my life. I needed to find myself again and put my life back together. I had to let go of the past and begin a new single, happy life. That's why I decided to write RESTORED: Connecting with God After Divorce because I was so lost and broken and living an ungodly life. I had to put God first in my life; not last!

With this book, you will easily find Scriptures that you can apply to your situation and grow closer to Christ. You don't have to walk this life alone. God is with you and His word is true. As you read this book and study in your Bible, you will be on your way to finding your purpose in life after divorce.

"FOR I KNOW THE PLANS I HAVE FOR YOU, SAYS THE LORD."

JEREMIAH 29:11 NLT

PLAN B

When I said my wedding vows, I meant every word. I never would have thought that after three and half years I would be throwing in the towel. I've never been a person to quit and here I am quitting on my marriage. It wasn't fun anymore. The arguing upset me and I just didn't feel valued in the relationship. Instead of working on things, I decided marriage wasn't for me. If things didn't go my way, I was done. I detached myself situations and moved on. It could be friends, work, hobbies and sadly my marriage. It took my divorce to show me that without God every decision I made was wrong.

Living without Christ in my life, made me see and react to things differently. I wasn't extending grace or showing mercy to those I cared about. I just wanted to live my life the way I wanted and the way I wanted was plan B. When God is not involved in our decision making, we are changing the plans he already has for us. Jeremiah 29:11 clearly states, *"For I know the plans I have for you,"* says the Lord. *"They are plans for good and not for disaster, to give you a future and a hope."* My plans were to control everything when I needed to follow the plans that God had for me instead. His ways are better than our ways. Now that I'm divorced, I've learned to trust in God and pray about everything. I know for some of you divorce might not have been what you wanted and perhaps you were blindsided by it. Though you may have been blindsided, God wasn't. God's plan will always prevail and he has a much better plan than you could ever dream of. Trust in his promises and let him lead the way!

JOURNAL

How did the scripture speak to you?

What can you work on this week to be a better version of you?

PRAYER NOTES

"DRAW CLOSE TO GOD, AND GOD WILL DRAW CLOSE
TO YOU."

JAMES 4:8 NLT

DON'T RUN AWAY

When you are hurting, it is easy to run and hide. You cut off friends and family and try to process what is going on. At times, you may even think that cutting off God is a good thing but that's when you need him even more. The pain you are going through isn't going to go away on its own. Hiding from God isn't going to help your situation or allow you to break free from bondage. The enemy loves to keep us in darkness. He wants you to continue to be in condemnation and depression. He doesn't want you to move on with your life. He knows that if he can keep you in misery, the further you will drift from God.

As his word says, *you must draw near to him and he will draw near to you.* When you are feeling like your life is over, call on God to see you through your heartache. Focus on his promises and stay in the Word. Don't let the enemy keep telling you lies where you can't trust God anymore. Satan wants you to believe you are unloved and unworthy and that God doesn't care. God cares about you and your pain. He knows what you are going through but he wants you to know that this too shall pass. You will get stronger and your days will get brighter. This hurt will **NOT** last forever. The sun will shine again but you have to believe that. You have to believe that God has not forgotten you and though this is something that you were not anticipating or wanting, he can change it for your good. Don't run away from your Heavenly Father. Allow him to fix your hurts so that you will see better days ahead!

JOURNAL

How did the scripture speak to you?

What can you work on this week to be a better version of you?

PRAYER NOTES

"*...POUR OUT YOUR HEART TO HIM...*"

PSALM 62:8 NLT

LET IT FLOW

Have you ever been angry with God and decided not to tell him? You are angry about your situation but instead of talking to God about it you decide to cry to all your friends. In the book of Job, we see that Job tried that with his friends and didn't get anywhere. His friends blamed him for all the things that were going on with him. Even his wife gave him bad advice. It wasn't until Job turned to God with his frustrations, that he got answers. See Job poured out his heart and soul to our Heavenly Father. He told him he didn't understand but he knew God would make everything all right. He knew everything that was given to him and taken, could all be replaced if God wanted to.

Job, David, Moses and so many others were not ashamed to cry out to the Father. They knew they could bring anything to God's feet and he would hear them. God doesn't want you to keep things bottled up. He wants you to come to him about everything. Even when you are hurting and you feel God has been unfair to you, let him know. Share your feelings with him. Don't feel like you will make God angry. He already knows how you feel. He knows you are upset and confused. You are his child and he loves you. It hurts him even more when you are in pain. Let him heal you. Let your tears fall and if you have to cry to him daily, that's what God is here for. He is your Comforter and Refuge. Let it flow and watch God turn your tears into joy!

JOURNAL

How did the scripture speak to you?

What can you work on this week to be a better version of you?

PRAYER NOTES

"YOUR WORD IS A LAMP TO MY FEET AND A LIGHT
FOR MY PATH."

PSALM 119:105 NLT

HE LIGHTS THE WAY

When I divorced, my son was two years old. I was overwhelmed with how I was going to raise him and give him a stable environment. How would I pay the bills? Where would we live? Questions just kept popping up in my head. Trying to manage this "new" life seemed daunting. I was now going to co-parent with my ex and try to stay sane all at the same time. It was a time in my life that I needed to depend on God and not myself. I wasn't going to be able to move forward with my life, if I didn't have God in it. Allowing God to lead the way, was the only answer. His light leads us down the right path. When God leads the way, you can't go wrong. I casted my cares to him and allowed him to work in my life. A few years after my divorce, I bought my first house. I never thought it would be possible as a single mother but all things are possible with God. Life may not look pretty right now, but things will change. Times will get better. Don't think because you are divorced that life is over. However difficult or challenging your divorce is or may have been, **it's not the end of the road**. You still have years remaining to let God shine his brightest light in your life. God can turn your messiness into greatness. Stay in the Word of God and let it refresh your soul!

JOURNAL

How did the scripture speak to you?

What can you work on this week to be a better version of you?

PRAYER NOTES

"CAN ALL YOUR WORRIES ADD A SINGLE MOMENT TO
YOUR LIFE? OF COURSE NOT."

MATTHEW 6:27 NLT

STOP WORRYING

It's hard not to worry when your life is uncertain. For so long, you had everything planned out. You lived with two incomes, the kids were okay and you lived in your house since college. Now, you have one income, the kids are shuttled back and forth and the house you once loved is sold. Your retirement fund has hit a snag, your hours have been cut at work due to school and sport functions for the kids and you're living back at your parents house. Every day seems to be one big headache and you're just trying to stay afloat. How can you stop worrying, right??

Well, for starters, because it is not going to change a thing. It's not going to add any time to your life. It's not going to make your circumstances go away and quite frankly, too much anxiety can be very unhealthy. God doesn't want you spending your days worrying about what's going to happen tomorrow or let alone the rest of your day. He wants you to fully rely on him and his promises. Living on your own for the first time in many years is scary. The world isn't going to stop for you because your life has changed. No matter how hard things may be, God is ready to help you through it. He will supply all you need. He will make a way out of no way. Of course, you will get anxious. We're human! There will be times where worrying is practical. It's when you stay in the place of worrying about everything that shows God you're not trusting him. Divorce is a huge change but it's nothing to keep you up at night when you have Jehovah Jireh on your side!

JOURNAL

How did the scripture speak to you?

What can you work on this week to be a better version of you?

PRAYER NOTES

"PRAY FOR THOSE WHO PERSECUTE YOU!"

MATTHEW 5:44 NLT

NOT MY ENEMY

Divorce can bring out the ugliness in people. The one you once loved and would do anything for, you can't even look at; let alone talk to them. It might even be so hurtful that you can't stand to even be around them. Your heart has broken into a million pieces and it seems that you will never be able to forgive your ex. You may be valid in those feelings that you have towards them, but is that any way to live? Can you honestly spend the rest of your life offended by what you or your ex did? If kids are involved, does the divorce have to hurt them anymore than it does by constantly degrading your ex or dragging out the divorce in court battles?

When Jesus was nailed to the cross and he saw and felt all the hatred around him, he asked the Father to forgive them because they didn't know what they were doing. He didn't look at them judgmentally or secretly ask the Father to take them around back! He showed them compassion and love. When you're hurting it's hard to express love and understanding. It's difficult to see the one you gave your all to move on with someone else, or leave you for no reason at all. It's challenging when your ex leaves you with nothing after you gave them twenty years of your life. How are you supposed to pray for them? You pray for them just like Christ did. You ask God to forgive them for the pain they caused you. You learn to see them not as the enemy, but someone who is broken and lost. Divorce isn't easy and at times can be suffocating, but God will heal those wounds. It begins when you can learn to see them beyond the offense!

JOURNAL

How did the scripture speak to you?

What can you work on this week to be a better version of you?

35

PRAYER NOTES

"AND THE HOLY SPIRIT HELPS US IN OUR
DISTRESS."

ROMANS 8:26 NLT

HE DOES CARE

Being a Christian I was under the impression that if I did everything right, my life would go smoothly. I thought if I honored my husband and followed the Word, I would have that fairytale marriage. When my marriage began to crumble, I wondered if God even cared for me? I was attending church regularly and I was beginning to apply what I learned to my life but in the end I still ended up getting a divorce. Where was God? Did he leave me? Did I do something wrong?

Years later, as I was putting my life together, good things just kept happening to my ex. He was getting promoted on his job and he remarried. What gives? Through my anguish and despair, it was hard to see God working in my life. Boy, was I sadly mistaken. Through all the tears and heartache, God was still there and he still cared for me just as he always has. God doesn't disappear when we're suffering. He is right beside you sharing in your pain. The Holy Spirit within us is giving us the strength to wake up every morning, take care of the kids and maintain our job. The Holy Spirit is continuously present even when it seems that he is not there. **God cares for you!** It may seem that the world is collapsing all around you, but believe with your whole heart that God is setting in motion the blessings that are yet to come. The distress you are feeling right now, will go away. Time heals everything and while the clock is still ticking God is carrying you through it all!

JOURNAL

How did the scripture speak to you?

What can you work on this week to be a better version of you?

PRAYER NOTES

"FOR ALL HAVE SINNED AND FALL SHORT OF GLORY
OF GOD"

ROMANS 3:23 NIV

FALLING EVERY DAY

The one question I got asked the most after my divorce was, "what did he do". It would've been great to say 'he cheated' since that was the only way to get out of the relationship in God's eyes but that wasn't the case. Any other reason was sin. Once we were joined together no man should tear us apart. Well, I was the man who tore it apart! I was emotionally drained in my marriage and I didn't see a way out. Instead of praying for God to help me in my marriage, I thought the best thing for me was to just leave. Start over. I intentionally sinned. I took matters into my own hands and broke free.

As I began to grow stronger in my Faith, I was ashamed of what I had done. I didn't see how God was going to forgive me for giving up on the man I thought I loved. Was God going to hold this against me forever? It started eating me up inside until I finally talked to a pastor at my church. She explained to me that my sin is not different from any other sin and we all fall short of the glory of God. The condemnation that I felt over my divorce made me feel that I was a horrible person. I had to learn that every day I am sinning in some sort of capacity. I had to realize that the sin of my divorce was forgiven when I asked. I didn't need to carry it around and feel tainted because I was a divorcee. If you are feeling the same, **let it go!** God loves you and he understands that we are going to make mistakes. As we continue to live in this fallen world, we will come up short again and again. Thank our Father for sending his beautiful son Jesus. He died on the cross for all of our sins including divorce. We may fall every day but we can trust in the One to pick us right back up!

JOURNAL

How did the scripture speak to you?

What can you work on this week to be a better version of you?

PRAYER NOTES

"RUN AWAY FROM SEXUAL SIN!"

1 CORINTHIANS 6:18 NLT

RUN, JUMP, HIDE

Being single again comes with a lot of sacrifices and the one that stands out the most is sex. You can't get away from it. It's in movies, television shows and talked about in commercials. You once had a thriving or at least once a month sex drive and now, you have to put it on hold. For how long you're probably thinking. Until you marry again? Until you date for a few months and then try it out? Well, my friend the verse up above is for you and me!

Sex isn't a sin unless you are married. Unfortunately, your ex doesn't count anymore. God is specifically telling us to run from the temptations that will cause us to stumble. Subjecting our bodies for personal gratification is not only dangerous but costly. Our bodies are where the Holy Spirit dwells. Sleeping around is a defilement of our temple. Our bodies were meant to honor God. While you may be thinking, you're already damaged goods, the sin of divorce has been erased and you are now on a clean slate. God wants you to wait until the new spouse arrives. Giving yourself to someone not only disrupts your emotions, but it can also cloud your judgment. You can't trust your emotions and sex, though we like to think it doesn't, brings on a whole spectrum of emotions; especially for women. I remember getting myself tied up with a guy that I had no business getting tied up in and I was blocking my blessings. I kept getting hurt over and over again because I kept sleeping around with the wrong men. God had to show me that I needed to stop and value my body he paid the price for. As I write this, it will be nearly ten years since my last sexual encounter. God has helped me control that desire. It was hard in the beginning but over time the temptation has worn off. That's what God will do. When you obey his Word, you won't have to run, jump and hide!

JOURNAL

How did the scripture speak to you?

What can you work on this week to be a better version of you?

PRAYER NOTES

"FOR GOD BOUGHT YOU WITH A HIGH PRICE. SO YOU MUST HONOR GOD WITH YOUR BODY"

1 CORINTHIANS 6:20 NLT

BOUGHT AT A PRICE

So you're probably thinking not another devotion about sex but yes, this is another one. God talked about sex throughout the whole Bible because it is something that he knew was difficult to obey. He stressed over and over again how powerful our sexuality is. Our bodies were not created for sexual immorality. Sex was designed to be enjoyed in marriage. Sadly for us, we are no longer married anymore and the perks of sex have been stripped away. Sex outside of marriage is considered fornication. It is one area in our lives that God despises. He sees it as gross negligence to our bodies. Our bodies should be treasured and valued. Celibacy is the only way while living single.

For some of you, this may not be an issue. You're trying to put your life back together and sex is the last thing on your mind. But for others, this may be a real concern and if it is, you're not alone. Ask God to help you if this is an area of weakness. God will never put more on us than we can bear but we have to be willing to do the work. Pray that God will give you strength to fight the temptation, stay in the Word and speak with fellow Christians to help you hold yourself accountable. Join other single Christians who are also trying to follow God's commands in staying celibate. One thing that has helped me, is to stay out of relationships. I am not wanting to marry anytime soon or perhaps ever again and dating wouldn't make sense. I've spent these years raising my son and focusing on my career and aspirations. Though this is my journey, it may look different for you. If you are in hopes to marry again, you will have to date. Keep your dates in groups or during the day. Find ways to date that will not hinder your walk with Christ. Persistent prayer is key to fighting temptations. Remember, that your body is priceless!

JOURNAL

How did the scripture speak to you?

What can you work on this week to be a better version of you?

PRAYER NOTES

*"AND I WANT WOMEN TO BE MODEST IN THEIR
APPEARANCE"*

1 TIMOTHY 2:9 NLT

WHAT YOU WEARIN'

I remember when I worked at a men's correctional facility. I was in my mid twenties and I had finally lost the weight from my pregnancy. I loved wearing heels (the higher the better) and pencil skirts. I was pretty fashionable. I didn't give much thought on how I dressed besides not showing too much skin. Cover the buns and keep the girls hidden. I thought that would be enough, right? My attire caused quite a stir at a job I had years ago. Complaints and rumors began to swarm. My supervisor even asked me to buy specific skirts!

It wasn't until I read what was in the Word that I realized the way I dressed dishonored who I was in Christ. My wardrobe became a temptation. I started thinking; if Jesus were to ask me out to dinner, would I wear the same thing? Would I feel comfortable walking in the temple without people gawking at me? When I started asking these questions, I knew something had to change. I didn't want guys getting the wrong impression of me. Our clothes play a huge role in how we're perceived. He wants us to be modest in our appearance. Just because you're not busting out of your shirt doesn't mean you're dressed appropriately. Our clothes should be fitted according to our shape, not too tight or baggy, chest and bottoms covered and above all, comfortable! Now, don't get me wrong, we don't have to dress like a nun or wear a sackcloth but keep in mind what attention it may bring. God did create our beautiful and unique bodies but keep the surprises for your next wedding day!

JOURNAL

How did the scripture speak to you?

What can you work on this week to be a better version of you?

PRAYER NOTES

"IF I WERE STILL TRYING TO PLEASE PEOPLE, I WOULD NOT BE A SERVANT OF CHRIST"

GALATIANS 1:10 NIV

NOT HERE TO PLEASE

Living a life in Christ can be difficult as a single person. People have so many opinions on how you should conduct your life now that you're not married anymore. The clothes you should wear, places you should hangout or who you should date. They constantly want to know what's going on in your life and why you're not moving on as quickly as they think you should. At times you may give in by trying to be nice but ultimately you just want to live your life. Let me tell you, that you don't have to listen to anybody but God. He is the only one you should be trying to please.

Ending a relationship is not easy. You have to deal with the grief of what happened and put your life back together again. You don't have to get back on the horse just because your best friend thinks it's time. Go at your own pace. Focus on yourself first and if you have kids, the primary focus should be on them. When I finally decided to live a celibate life, some of my friends thought it was crazy. The thought of not having sex for an extended amount of time seemed foreign to them. It became a topic of discussion that was not only annoying but judgmental. I had to put their ideas in the back of my mind because I knew it was the enemy trying to tempt me. The enemy wanted me to see how foolish it was to go without sex but he was wrong. When you live to please God you can get through **ANYTHING**. Pleasing God may not always be the fun or "normal" thing to do in our society but it is totally worth it in the end!

How did the scripture speak to you?

What can you work on this week to be a better version of you?

PRAYER NOTES

"THE IMPORTANT THING IS TO KEEP GOD'S
COMMANDMENTS"

1 CORINTHIANS 7:19 NLT

KEEPING HIS COMMANDS

When the going gets tough, it's easy to want to take a shortcut. The marriage has failed and you have to start making decisions on your own. The things you used to do while married, have now changed. Your tithing at the church has become sporadic, the Bible hasn't been opened in months and your communication with the Father has slowed. Your life begins to look like a trainwreck because while you're trying to put the pieces back together, you are forgetting about the One person who has the missing piece! Though divorce may not be an ideal situation that God would like to see you in, it doesn't mean that he doesn't care. Keeping his commandments after divorce is just as important as it was while you were married.

Our security isn't based on whether we are married or not. God will supply all of your needs and more. Withholding your tithes because of fear that you won't have enough to pay your bills is not only unwise but unbiblical. God says to bring your first tenth to the storehouse every month whether you lost income or not. Again, God knows your heart and what you're going through but if you honor him by following his commands, life will be easier. Continue to read the Word even if it's only five minutes a day. Keep the line of communication open to him because he wants to hear from you. As a single mother, I used to struggle giving more than my tithes. If extra money came in I would use it for things that we needed or wanted. It wasn't until God laid on my heart about blessing others. I started giving beyond my tithes to charities or missions that I knew would help those in need and you know, God still continued to bless me! I know how hard it is having to start over but when you keep God first and follow his commands, all the rest will fall into place!

JOURNAL

How did the scripture speak to you?

What can you work on this week to be a better version of you?

PRAYER NOTES

"SO DON'T GET TIRED OF DOING WHAT'S GOOD"

GALATIANS 6:9 NLT

KEEP DOING GOOD

In 2009, I received one of the biggest blows of my life when I found out my ex was having a baby from our son's preschool teacher. Apparently, my son was keeping this secret and shared it with the class. The concerned teacher then told me and I confronted my ex. Of course, at first, he denied the news but later came clean. He thought telling me the news would make me stop allowing him to see our son since I had sole custody. Though I was hurt on how quickly their relationship blossomed, I wasn't going to prevent my son from seeing his father. I hear so many stories where former spouses or partners want to be vindictive and involve the kids in their issues. What they don't understand is that it only hurts the kids. The kids don't deserve to be put in compromising situations. I told my ex that what he did was wrong and as far as I know that hasn't happened again!

A couple years after his child was born, he was in need of a babysitter because he was going through marital issues with his second wife. I had just quit my job and had nothing planned so I volunteered. Yes, the child he so desperately tried to hide, was the same child I helped watch for at least two years! His son had nothing to do with our personal issues and he was our son's brother. It allowed them time to bond and it showed the love of Christ. If my relationship with God wasn't as strong, I don't know if I would have been able to do it given everything I had been through with him. God showed me that doing good is always better than just being upset or holding a grudge. My ex was going through a difficult time and by God's grace and goodness he placed me in a position that I could help out. Being good doesn't stop because we are hurting or thrown into a situation we didn't expect but with God's help anything is possible!

JOURNAL

How did the scripture speak to you?

What can you work on this week to be a better version of you?

PRAYER NOTES

"TEACH US TO MAKE THE MOST OF OUR TIME SO
THAT WE MAY GROW IN WISDOM"

PSALM 90:12 NLT

SPENDING TIME WISELY

Do your days seem longer? You go to work and go home and then nothing. You sit on the couch binging the latest show on Netflix while munching on the newest flavor of Ben & Jerry's ice cream. You seemed to have lost your purpose and life seems boring. You're spending your time on things that aren't bringing any fruit to your life. Well, it's time to get off the couch and do something productive. God didn't create us to sit around and wait for the next best opportunity. Every day we have on this earth is a blessing and we should be using it to bring him glory. Find ways to start using your time wisely and advancing his Kingdom.

Maybe you could join a small group or bible study, volunteer at a shelter, or find a new hobby. Whatever you decide to do, do it on the basis of honoring your Heavenly Father. Maybe mentoring teens at your church or starting a book club can be a way to start using your time effectively. When we start getting complacent in our lives, God can't use us. You may be missing an opportunity to bless or speak the Word of Christ to someone because you may be focusing on the wrong things. Now, there is nothing wrong with watching Netflix, I mean as I'm writing this I can't wait to see season four of Cobra Kai, but it does become a problem when you don't want to do anything else but sit in front of the television all weekend or shopping online. It's not only unproductive but wasteful of the time that God has given you on this earth. Remember, God still has a purpose for you and it starts with using your time wisely!

JOURNAL

How did the scripture speak to you?

What can you work on this week to be a better version of you?

PRAYER NOTES

"NOW LET ME BRING YOU THIS COMPLAINT: WHY
ARE THE WICKED SO PROSPEROUS? WHY ARE EVIL
PEOPLE SO HAPPY"

JEREMIAH 12:1 NLT

BRING IT ON

Have you ever silently been upset when you hear or see a non-believer or a lukewarm Christian thriving? The late coworker gets promoted, an atheist becomes the latest millionaire on Forbes list or your neighbor comes home with another Tesla. All around, you see the blessings continue to pour in. It seems never ending as your circumstances stand still or keep getting worse. As you try to put on a smile and carry-on, you steadily wonder what's going on in your own life. You're constantly doing the right things but you still seem stuck in the mud. The question is inevitable. Why God? Why are those who don't love you as much as I do, keep getting blessed. Why am I struggling to make ends meet while my ex is happily remarried? God, are you still mad at me?

You're not doing anything wrong and it's okay to ask the Father or express your complaints to him. He wants you to bring it to him! Jeremiah, Job and Asaph all brought their concerns to God. They all cried out on how the wicked seemed to be living so well as they suffered through their trials. I remember crying out to God one afternoon in tears on how my life seemed to be going nowhere as my ex-husband's life seemed to be flourishing. I thought to myself, what gives? He revealed to me that he can bless whoever he chooses and I had to learn to be content in any situation. It's none of our business who he blesses or not! It's his timing not ours when he decides to bless us. I thanked God for his mercy and continuous provisions. By sharing my heart, he let me know that he cares. If you're feeling some kind of way about something, lay it at the Father's feet. Tell him and then let it go. God knows your heart and he can handle whatever you have to bring, so bring it!

JOURNAL

How did the scripture speak to you?

What can you work on this week to be a better version of you?

PRAYER NOTES

"ABOVE ALL ELSE, GUARD YOUR HEART, FOR IT
AFFECTS EVERYTHING YOU DO"

PROVERBS 4:23 NLT

GUARD YOUR HEART

Guarding your heart isn't about not dating anymore or being closed off to getting married again. It's about cleansing yourself from anything that could be impure. The thoughts you keep to yourself about others that aren't pleasant could potentially slip out when you're at a moment of weakness. That's why God explains that your tongue is a double edged sword. It can bring blessings or curses. That's why your heart is so important not to keep hatred or bitterness because what flows in the heart will eventually spew out from the tongue. You may think, that's not me, but have you taken inventory of your heart? How do you feel about your ex? How do you feel about their new wife? Are you bad-mouthing him to your friends? Are you constantly criticizing your ex's new spouse? These feelings are not of God.

God wants you to relinquish any pain you had with your ex and learn to love them as God does. Holding on to the hurts of your past will only fester in your heart. The ugly feelings you have of them will undoubtedly find a way out if you don't deal with the issue right away. Ask God to help you to love those who have offended you. Allow God to cleanse your heart and your mind by studying his Word. A good book to read is Hosea. Hosea was commanded to marry Gomer who was the town prostitute. He loved her so much but her transgressions were too much for him to bear. God helped him in seeing Gomer as he saw her. Eventually he took her back and he learned to accept Gomer for who she is. It may not be easy moving on when someone you loved has hurt you so deeply. The pain can cripple you at times and being nice to those who cause the pain is probably last on your list. Guarding your heart takes time and a whole lot of patience but with God he can help keep those feelings at bay if you allow him to help!

How did the scripture speak to you?

What can you work on this week to be a better version of you?

PRAYER NOTES

"HATRED STIRS UP CONFLICT, BUT LOVE COVERS
OVER ALL WRONGS"

PROVERBS 10:12 NIV

STOP THE HATE

It may seem unfathomable to see celebrities in a bad light but they're human just like you. They go through the same trials you do but for them, the whole world is watching. It seems like every week you hear about another famous couple headed for divorce. Some have been going through divorce for years continuously fighting over child custody, property assets or spousal support. You begin to realize their life is no different than your own. You keep delaying the court proceedings or refuse to give up something that doesn't matter. Is it worth putting the kids through drama because you don't want your ex to have anything at all? No matter the iniquities that were revealed in your marriage that have now caused you both to go your separate ways, you don't have to hate them while you are in the process of moving on.

When I decided to leave my husband, I wanted the least resistance. I didn't want him to challenge me on anything and I gave up a lot so that I could get on with my life. I didn't want our two year old son dealing with our drama. I wanted him to see us in the best light possible and if I started off right we could learn to co-parent positively. I may have given up a lot, but I got what was important to me; sole custody of my son. Sometimes, we have to look at the bigger picture and choose our battles wisely. When we act out of a place of love and not hate, God will help us move on faster. God can't use you if you're wallowing in hatred. Let God's love cover you and watch the hate slip away!

JOURNAL

How did the scripture speak to you?

What can you work on this week to be a better version of you?

PRAYER NOTES

"A RELAXED ATTITUDE LENGTHENS LIFE; JEALOUSY
ROTS IT AWAY"

PROVERBS 14:30 NLT

JEALOUS OF WHO?

When your life's falling apart it's hard to find peace. It's tough trying to find the happiness that you once had. You used to be able to attend the country club, have game night with other couples and have romantic getaways. Now you have to work long hours, rearrange your work schedule for sporting events and balance your budget off of one income. It's easy to get resentful or envious of those around you. Your friends' marriages are still thriving and you can barely hold it together. They tell you all the exciting things going on in their lives and you have to bite your lip just to force a smile. Before you know it, jealousy starts to seep in.

Jealousy is a trick from the devil. He is making you believe that your life isn't good enough and everyone else has a better life than you. Your road may be difficult at this time but don't let the enemy steal your joy. The enemy will put thoughts in your head and make you feel envious and resentful about your situation but go to God. Let him strengthen you and repair your broken heart. Your heart is aching but don't let it fool you into thinking that your life doesn't matter. Your ex may have already moved on and created a new life but don't let it get to you. I know how challenging it is to see the one you once loved have everything going right while you're still putting two and two together. Trust that what God has for you is better than the season you're in. God will turn your mess into a blessing but don't let jealousy hold you back!

JOURNAL

How did the scripture speak to you?

What can you work on this week to be a better version of you?

PRAYER NOTES

"YOU MUST MAKE ALLOWANCE FOR EACH OTHER'S FAULTS AND FORGIVE THE PERSON WHO OFFENDS YOU"

COLOSSIANS 3:13 NLT

UNLOAD FORGIVENESS

I remember when Kathie Lee Gifford was publicly humiliated by the admission of her now late husband having an affair. The media was being the media and everyone wanted to know what she was going to do. As a firm believer, she relied on her faith in God and saved her marriage. Many people were shocked and thought she was crazy to stay with him. She decided to forgive him while the world wanted to crucify him. Her choice to forgive him showed the secular world that the faults of others deserve to be forgiven. What he did was wrong and no one could fault her if she did decide to leave. It is a personal decision but whatever choice you make, forgiveness must be key. Whatever offenses that were made during your divorce, you must forgive not only your ex but forgive yourself as well.

Forgiveness isn't about accepting the offense or letting someone off the hook. It's about releasing the negative energy that's taken over you. Forgiving releases that power. You're able to put your life back together when you forgive those that have trespassed against you. However egregious the offense may have been to you, it's nothing compared to the greatest offense that was bestowed upon our savior Jesus Christ when he was nailed to the cross. He was tortured, flogged and mocked for being the Messiah and yet he forgave those who persecuted him. As he died on the cross, he cried out to the Father saying, *"Father, forgive them, for they do not know what they are doing."* His example that day shows how important and necessary it is to forgive so the healing process can begin. Forgiveness isn't always an easy thing but once you make it a habit to forgive quickly, the sooner God can't get you on your way!

JOURNAL

How did the scripture speak to you?

What can you work on this week to be a better version of you?

PRAYER NOTES

"SHE IS CLOTHED WITH STRENGTH AND DIGNITY;
SHE CAN LAUGH AT THE DAYS TO COME"

PROVERBS 31:25 NIV

STRENGTH AND HONOR

The Proverbs 31 woman is a woman we all strive to be. She is supportive, loving and confident. She wants the best for her family and she takes pride in who she is in Christ. She's not concerned with the cares of the world and she doesn't put up with any attitudes. She is the epitome of strength and honor. Fortunately for her, she didn't have to deal with social media, back-stabbing friends, rambunctious kids or a philandering spouse. She also never had to sit in front of a judge wiping away tears as he read off your divorce decree. She was "perfect".

After reading Proverbs 31, you probably felt like she was perfect. That she had it altogether. God says only one on this earth was perfect and his name is Jesus. Jesus is the only human being who will ever be perfect. The Proverbs 31 woman wasn't written so that we could put her on a pedestal. God didn't disclose everything about her but I know for sure she had times of inadequacies. She had times of sadness, doubt and possibly insecurities. God chose to show the best of her so that you can be the best you can be. She exemplified everything that God wants to see in your growth as a Christian woman. Though she was married, it was her character God wanted you to see. You may not be married anymore but your strength is still within you. You are loved by the Most High and were created for a purpose. You may not be living the life of the Proverbs 31 woman but rest assured no one is. Take what you can from her and make it your **OWN**. You are clothed in strength and honor, my friend, and you can laugh away any nonsense you may be facing, because better days are yet to come!

JOURNAL

How did the scripture speak to you?

What can you work on this week to be a better version of you?

PRAYER NOTES

"FOR WE ARE GOD'S MASTERPIECE"

EPHESIANS 2:10 NLT

HIS MASTERPIECE

You know, divorce has a way of making you feel less than. You spent so much time in a relationship that you thought was going to last only to end up single again. Whether you're recently divorced or it's been awhile, you may be asking yourself "what now" or "who am I"? The enemy wants you to believe that you have nothing to give anymore now that you're "damaged goods". He wants you to think you have no purpose and should sit in your room and sulk. Just because your marriage has ended doesn't mean your life is over!

Hear this, you are God's masterpiece! You were created by the finest hands and with the most precious clay there is. You are his unique and special pot. Each and everyone of us, was made by his touch and he created each *"pot"* for a specific purpose. Your divorce doesn't define who you are. In Gods' eyes, he still smiles every time you wake up. He cries every time you cry and he laughs when you laugh. Words may have been exchanged that were hurtful when you divorced but those words are not true. What God thinks of you is all that matters. He wants you to see yourself as an exquisite jar of clay. He molded you just the way you are. You may not do everything he says and you will continue to fall short, but at the end of the day, he will never regret the day he made you. As long as you still have breath in your lungs, your work for his Kingdom isn't done. Some may think you're worthless but to him, you are everything!

JOURNAL

How did the scripture speak to you?

What can you work on this week to be a better version of you?

PRAYER NOTES

"HE HEALS THE BROKENHEARTED, BINDING UP
THEIR WOUNDS"

PSALM 147:3 NLT

HIS HEALING POWER

A few years after my divorce, I met someone that I thought could be the "one". He was great with my son, he made me laugh and liked to dance. My emotions ran faster than I could see that he honestly wasn't the one for me. There were red flags but I decided to ignore them. After a few months of dating, he called it off. I was blindsided and hurt. It was the first time I had let my heart open again and I was heartbroken. The hardest part wasn't moving on but my son asking where he had gone. Ouch!! My son asking for my ex-boyfriend was a hard pill to swallow. I broke down and cried.

In those tears, God spoke to my heart. The relationship I was seeking was not with him, but with *Him*. The day he broke up with me, I was already a few days into my first 21 day fast. God removed all the negativity that would've kept me from hearing him. The pain of an ended relationship, dissipated quickly as I continued to dive into the Word and rest in God's hands. He comforted me like never before. I felt the weight of God surrounding me like a blanket. His loving power healed my broken heart. If your wounds need to be healed, call on the Father. Let his healing power free you of your pain and suffering. Our hearts may be fragile but our mind is strong. Study his Word and let the words of his promises comfort you. Allow his power to restore the strength you once had. Tears may be falling now, but joy comes in the morning. Let the power of his healing touch begin in you now!

JOURNAL

How did the scripture speak to you?

What can you work on this week to be a better version of you?

PRAYER NOTES

"DON'T THINK ONLY ABOUT YOUR OWN AFFAIRS ,
BUT BE INTERESTED IN OTHERS, TOO, AND WHAT
THEY ARE DOING"

PHILIPPIANS 2:4 NLT

ENOUGH CRYING

Joyce Meyer has coined the phrase, "get yourself off yourself". I think that is the best medicine when you are getting down on yourself. When you think all about your problems, how are you able to help anyone else around you? God needs you to bless someone and you're sitting in your room pouting. It's time to let go of the pity party. Enough crying! God can't use you if you're wrapped up in your own circumstances. When you have done all you can, you have to let God do the rest. Crying over spilled milk isn't going to wipe the milk up. Eventually you're going to have to get the paper towel and clean up the mess. The judge has stamped the divorce decree and you're officially divorced. No more milk to clean up.

Now, I understand you will have bad days. God understands that as well, but in those bad days, find something to do. Volunteer at a hospital or shelter, call a friend and see how they're doing, take a walk or just ask God what to do. He will show you ways to be a blessing to someone else. Maybe he wants you to share your testimony to someone or mentor young adults at church. There are so many things you can do to occupy your time. Nothing is worse than feeling and being alone after a divorce. Unless you have kids, the emptiness you feel is debilitating. Relieve that emptiness by focusing on others around you. Don't let your tears keep you in the house all day. Freshen up and start living your life again. You'll be happy you did!

JOURNAL

How did the scripture speak to you?

What can you work on this week to be a better version of you?

PRAYER NOTES

"FOR OUR PEOPLE SHOULD NOT HAVE UNPRODUCTIVE LIVES"

TITUS 3:14 NLT

STAY PRODUCTIVE

Boy, isn't it easy to start feeling sorry for yourself? You're having car issues, the bills are piling up and work has become unbearable. Sometimes you just feel like throwing in the towel and giving up. Your energy and positivity has ceased to exist and self-pity has taken over. You know who loves to see you this way? The enemy. He loves self-pity. He loves to see you miserable and ready to give up. While you think it's no big deal, the enemy is at work. The enemy starts to fill your mind with doubt and confusion. The lies he keeps whispering in your ear, has now made you want to stay home. Every day. You no longer want to do anything but stay in your room after work. The problem is, that is exactly where the enemy wants you. Curled up in your room having a pity party because he knows the less you can do for God the better it is for him. Don't let him win!

When you feel like self-pity has started to take over, you have to rise above it. You have to shake it off and find something to do. This is a great time to reach out to friends and family or pick up a good book. When you start to let your mind wander, the enemy can play his games. Staying productive helps eliminate the temptation to self condemnation. Crying every now and again or catching up on the latest episode of Flip or Flop, isn't going to break you. It's when it's all you want to do. You stop hanging with your friends, calling family members or even spending time with the kids. When that happens, my friend, it's a warning sign to get up and start moving. God has created you to serve. When you stop serving and focus on yourself and your problems, it opens the door to the enemy but when you stay productive and focus on the good in your life, you'll be sure to feel God's love all around you!

JOURNAL

How did the scripture speak to you?

What can you work on this week to be a better version of you?

PRAYER NOTES

"YET IF I LIVE, THAT MEANS FRUITFUL SERVICE FOR CHRIST"

PHILIPPIANS 1:22 NLT

LIVING FOR HIM

When you're married, you have to balance your spiritual life with your personal life. You have to be the supportive spouse and compromise with each other. You don't have much time to dedicate to Christ and he understands that. He created marriage and family but when it falls apart, it's no better time than to devote your life all over again to the One who created you. Of course, when you were married it didn't mean that you didn't live for Christ but you honored him every day by keeping your vows and taking care of your family. Now that you have more time, that time can be used to be more fruitful to our Heavenly Father.

You can lean on God more to guide your steps on servicing those around you that may need to be blessed. You can volunteer more at church, take up bible study or help other divorcees to overcome their divorce. There are so many ways you could be living for Christ each and every day. Ask God to help you in this area. Ask him to show you where the need is great and where you can be assistance. Every breath that you take is a gift from God. Though times may be tough after a tumultuous divorce, your life isn't over! Use your testimony to be a blessing to someone else who needs to hear it. Sometimes you will go through things that you don't understand but God knows everything. He has left you on this earth for a specific purpose. When you focus on the promises that God has made to you, living for him in a new way may be the breakthrough you have been waiting for!

JOURNAL

How did the scripture speak to you?

What can you work on this week to be a better version of you?

PRAYER NOTES

*"ALL THE WHILE, YOU WILL LEARN TO KNOW GOD
BETTER AND BETTER"*

COLOSSIANS 1:10 NLT

KNOW HIM BETTER

Discerning the will for your life takes effort. You can't just know what to do unless you know who God is and that can only be done by knowing the Word. When you immerse yourself into the Bible, you have a better understanding of who God is and why you are here. The words on the pages are not just words to read and put away but words that must be followed and obeyed. The devotional before this 'Living For Him' shows your willingness to serve him in every area of your life. When you put your trust and faith in Christ, the more you begin to know who he is. You don't put your faith in strangers, do you? If someone you don't know were to ask you to invest in their company, you would be suspicious. You would want to know more about him and his business, right? That is what you have to do in your walk with Christ.

You must first begin to know the heart of God. When you start to know his heart, you will then start to trust him and want to do for him. You begin to apply what you have read in the Bible to your life and your life becomes more fruitful. When you honor God with your life, he is pleased. You will have spiritual wisdom the more you get to know the Father. You won't have to second guess yourself anymore. You will rely on the Word of God and put things into motion. The spiritual gifts God has placed in you will be ignited because you are forming a relationship with him. God doesn't want to be a master over your life. You are not his slave. He wants to have a loving, open and honest relationship with you. That's why we have the Bible. The more you know, the more you grow and the more you grow the more you will do for his Kingdom!

JOURNAL

How did the scripture speak to you?

What can you work on this week to be a better version of you?

PRAYER NOTES

"KEEP ON PRAYING"

1 THESSALONIANS 5:17 NLT

STAY PRAYERFUL

When I was younger, I thought that reciting my nightly prayers was my only way of communicating to God. I thought by reciting that exact prayer was all I had to do. It wasn't until I was older and walking with Christ on my own that prayers were basically just talking with God. Not just praying before bed or when an emergency came up, but whenever I felt like it. Prayer is not about walking around all day long talking to God but keeping him in the loop. Prayer should be your first thought and not your last. It can be where you set a specific time each day or when you know you won't be distracted as much. Staying prayerful, keeps the communication alive.

When I used to work a 9-5 job, I would pray during my commute to and from work. It was the time I knew that it would be uninterrupted. Now that I have more free time, I find myself talking to him a few times a day! Whatever is on my mind, I take it to him. Whether I'm happy, sad or just curious about something, I bring it to the Father. I used to think some pastors were saying I needed to talk to God for hours or have something extravagant to say. That's not true at all. Sometimes it could be as simple as *"Thank you, God"* or reciting scripture, *"I can do all things through Christ who strengthens me"*. When you stay prayerful, it's letting God know where he places in your life. You are letting him know he is not just a genie you call on for emergencies but a Father that you love and want involved in your life at all times!

JOURNAL

How did the scripture speak to you?

What can you work on this week to be a better version of you?

PRAYER NOTES

"CLING TIGHTLY TO YOUR FAITH IN CHRIST, AND ALWAYS KEEP YOUR CONSCIENCE CLEAR"

1 TIMOTHY 1:19 NLT

HOLD ON TIGHT

I have to admit that sometimes it's difficult to hold on to my Faith. When I see injustices or when I see an unbeliever get something I thought I should have, it bothers me. Sometimes I allow the enemy to put thoughts in my head when I get upset and enjoy the brief moment of the fantasy he plays. Thoughts of getting revenge and sometimes, pain to another. For that short moment, my faith goes away and I wonder if I could have a "pass". A pass not to be a Christian for a moment and allow the enemy to do his dirty work. The thoughts don't happen often, **THANKFULLY**, but when it does, I feel lost. Sometimes the pain can be so great, I wonder where is God? When I get like that, the more I have to press into my faith and clear my conscience.

If I allow my mind to get too lost in despair, the enemy can use that temptation for action. He hasn't won that fight because I cling to my faith as tight as I can. When those feelings rise up, I stop and pray. I begin to start thanking him for where he has me and that I'm still here for another day. I remind myself that whatever is going on in my life, this too shall pass. My trials will not last forever. The pain and injustices that I see in my country will not last forever. God reassures me that my destination is Heaven. It is a place where I will not have these feelings anymore or have to endure what I'm going through now. When you hold on to your faith, God will see you through. The enemy can't take the joy that God has placed in your heart. He may try to shake you up here on earth, but we serve a Greater God. Your faith alone will carry you through **ANYTHING**. As the 90's hit song by Wilson Phillips goes *"...hold on for one more day. Things will go your way."* Hang on my friend!

JOURNAL

How did the scripture speak to you?

What can you work on this week to be a better version of you?

PRAYER NOTES

"BUT AS FOR YOU, PROMOTE THE KIND OF LIVING
THAT REFLECTS RIGHT TEACHING"

TITUS 2:1

REFLECTION OF HIM

As you go about your daily life, you can get sidetracked by the kids, spouse, work or other engagements. You get lost on how your character is influencing those around you, especially unbelievers. You may be tense, short tempered or flustered by your long work hours and hectic schedule that you model poor behavior. Yelling at the kids or telling little fibs can be misconstrued that the behavior is acceptable. It is especially difficult to model exemplary behavior after going through a stormy divorce. You may start talking about your ex at work or your friends at happy hour. All of this may seem trivial but if we are to reflect our Savior at all times, this is something that must be addressed.

As the saying goes, everybody is watching, and that includes unbelievers. They can't wait to throw shade and call Christians hypocrites when we look less than perfect. They forget that we are all humans and that we will all fall short of the glory of God but unbelievers don't understand that. It gives them the excuse that they can continue to live the way they live. If we aren't reflecting the goodness of God and only showing our short fuse, who are they really seeing? The enemy wants us to model behavior after him so that it confuses those that aren't walking with Christ. It's a tactic he tries often, but as long as you take a look in the mirror from time to time and realize that sometimes your behavior is less than stellar, ask forgiveness and get back on track. When you model yourself for Christ, others will see *Him* in you. Even the most stubborn unbeliever will see the right teaching in you and prayerfully want to follow suit!

JOURNAL

How did the scripture speak to you?

What can you work on this week to be a better version of you?

PRAYER NOTES

Shauntae Spaulding is a Christian author who inspires to help others with words. This is her third published book and she hopes to bring more books to help empower women in their walk with Christ. As a divorced woman, she knows the challenges single women face in a secular world. The reliance on Jesus is ever more profound than ever before! Women must support and encourage each other to be the best version of themselves with God's grace and unconditional love.

She enjoys being outdoors taking long walks or hiking in the San Fernando Valley. She loves to watch action movies and spending time with family and friends.

9 798218 369163